classic moments

Fifty years of modern music.

Text by

Alan di Perna

Published by HAL LEONARD CORPORATION

7777 West Bluemound Road

P.O. Box 13819

Milwaukee, Wisconsin 53213

ISBN 0-7935-5591-4

ISBN 0-7935-5592-2 (Limited Edition)

Acknowledgments

Thanks to Brad Tolinski of *Guitar World* for introducing me to the Hal Leonard crew, to Alan Paul of *Guitar World* for SRV

tribute info, to Jeff Mayer for Jimmy Page and Police info, to Dwight Doerr and Jim Cruickshank of Fender for guidance and

support, and to Brad Smith of Hal Leonard for impeccable photo research, humor, and diplomacy. Maximum thanks to my wife

Robin for invaluable research and editorial assistance, and endless love.

Photo Credits

Front Cover and 3 (foreground), 94–95: Courtesy Fender Musical Instruments. Front Cover and 3 (far left), 41: MICHAEL OCHS ARCHIVES/Venice, CA. Front Cover and 3 (left), 16: © Ray Flerlage/MICHAEL OCHS ARCHIVES/Venice, CA. Front Cover and 3 (right), 108 (left); Front Cover and 3 (far right), 83: Courtesy Fender Musical Instruments. 11, 12–13: Courtesy Don and Gary Don Rhodes. 13: Courtesy Richard R. Smith, from *Fender: The Sound Heard 'round the World* (Garfish Publishing). 14: Courtesy George Fullerton. 14–15, 15: Courtesy Rita Shamblin. 17: Fender 1956–57 catalog, courtesy John Teagle. 18–19: Jimmy Velvet. 20: MICHAEL OCHS ARCHIVES/Venice, CA. 20–21: Courtesy John Teagle. 22: Jimmy Velvet. 22–23: © John Beecher/MICHAEL OCHS ARCHIVES/Venice, CA. 23 (top): MICHAEL OCHS ARCHIVES/Venice, CA. 23 (inset): Courtesy George Fullerton. 24: MICHAEL OCHS ARCHIVES/Venice, CA. 25: © Terry Cryer/FABIAN JOLIVET ARCHIVES. 26 (top): Frank Driggs Collection. 26 (bottom): MICHAEL OCHS ARCHIVES/Venice, CA. 27: Courtesy Fender Musical Instruments. 29: MICHAEL OCHS ARCHIVES/Venice, CA. 30, 31: Frank Driggs Collection. 32, 32–33, 34: MICHAEL OCHS ARCHIVES/Venice, CA.

35 (main): Courtesy Earl Van Dyke. 35 (inset): Courtesy Annie Jamerson. 36: Courtesy Hal Blaine. 37: Frank Driggs Collection. 38: MICHAEL OCHS ARCHIVES/Venice, CA. 39: © Alice Ochs/MICHAEL OCHS ARCHIVES/Venice, CA. 42–43: Fender Albums of Stars, courtesy John Teagle. 44: Frank Driggs Collection. 44–45: MICHAEL OCHS ARCHIVES/Venice, CA. 45: Barry Wentzell/STAR FILE. 46 (top): MICHAEL OCHS ARCHIVES/Venice, CA. 46 (left): © Jeffrey Mayer. 47: Frank Driggs Collection. 48: Michael Putland/RETNA LTD. 49: LGI. 50: MICHAEL OCHS ARCHIVES/Venice, CA. 51: © Apple Corps Ltd. 53: MICHAEL OCHS ARCHIVES/Venice, CA. 54: Dagmar/STAR FILE. 55 (left): Courtesy Carol Kaye. 55 (right): © Bob Cavallo. 56, 57: © Robb Lawrence. 58, 59: Courtesy James Burton International Fan Club. 60: Dagmar/STAR FILE. 61: Andy Freeberg/RETNA LTD. 62: © Robb Lawrence. 63: © Jon Sievert/MICHAEL OCHS ARCHIVES/Venice, CA. 64: Neil Zlozower. 65: © Jeffrey Mayer. 66: Chris Walter/RETNA LTD. 67: Chuck Pulin/STAR FILE. 68: © David Corio/MICHAEL OCHS ARCHIVES/Venice, CA. 69: Stevenson/RETNA LTD. 70: Jeffrey Mayer/STAR FILE. 71: Barry

Schultz/RETNA LTD. 73: LGI Stock. 74: © Jeffrey Mayer. 74–75: © Larry Hulst/MICHAEL OCHS ARCHIVES/Venice, CA. 76: © Mark Harlan/STAR FILE. 77: Gary Geshoff/RETNA LTD. 78: © Chris Walter/RETNA LTD. 79: © John Bellissimo/LGI. 80–81: Chuck Pulin/STAR FILE. 82: © Jay Blakesberg/RETNA LTD. 86: David Seelig/STAR FILE. 87: Courtesy Joe Barden. 88: Rick Gould/ICP. 88–89: © Joe Hughes/MICHAEL OCHS ARCHIVES/Venice, CA. 90–91: San Francisco Chronicle. 91: Busacca/RETNA LTD. 92, 93: Chuck Pulin/STAR FILE. 94: © Sandra Johnson/RETNA LTD. 96: Chuck Pulin/STAR FILE. 97: Jeffrey Mayer/STAR FILE. 98: Courtesy Paramount Pictures. 99 (left): Bucky Barrett. 99 (right): © Jeffrey Mayer. 100: © Lori Stoll/RETNA LTD. 100–101: © Lissa Wales. 101: Pat Enyart. 102: Courtesy Aggressive Entertainment. 103: Charles Peterson. 104: © Jeffrey Mayer. 105 (main photo): Jon Cohan. 105 (inset): Neal Preston/RETNA LTD. 106 (left): © Marty Perez/LGI. 106 (right): © Steve Eichner/RETNA LTD. 107: © Lance Mercer/RETNA LTD. 108 (right): © Rick Gould/ICP. 109: © Cindy Light/LGI. Dust Jacket (rear flap): Robin Lee Zarin.

Design and Illustration Monfre/Acott Design, Inc. Milwaukee, Wisconsin

table of contents

Depiction of artists in this book does not necessarily imply an endorsement of Fender Musical Instruments.

They were merely caught in a historical moment with the instrument of their choice at that time.

To Fender players everywhere, and to all Fender employees past and present, without whom these classic moments could never have happened.

Introduction

Born at the midpoint of the 20th century, Fender Musical Instruments was the first truly modern guitar company. Right from the start, Fender made instruments for the brave new world that was taking shape in the years just after World War II. In their design aesthetic, their sound, their methods of manufacture, and their marketing, Fender instruments belong to our time. And as we prepare to enter a brand-new century, many of the Fender "classics" seem as current as ever. Here in 1996—Fender's 50th Anniversary year—these innovative designs have become the benchmarks by which other instruments are assessed.

Fender instruments have had a profound impact on popular music in the latter half of this century. In turn, the continuing development of Fender guitars, basses, and amps has been shaped by the many gifted artists who have played them throughout the years, making Fender a part of their own personal styles.

That's what this book is about—the unique relationship that exists between artist, instrument, and audience. There are occasions when these three come together to create something unforgettable—a moment that enriches pop music culture and changes it forever. That's what we mean by a Fender Classic Moment.

Thanks to another great modern art form—photography—many of these moments have been preserved for us to savor today. Next to plugging in a Fender and cutting loose, what better way could there be to celebrate Fender's 50th Birthday?

It was a time of unbridled optimism. A new Age of Innocence, in many ways. America had emerged triumphant from the Great Depression and Second World War. There was a sense that the hard times were over. The post-war economy was booming. Opportunities were plentiful for entrepreneurs and inventors of every stripe. Americans were looking forward to a good long spell of prosperity, unprecedented personal comfort, and a wealth of leisure-time diversions. A great migration to the suburbs was underway. There was a brand-new thing called television. And a sleek, Jet Age design aesthetic was streamlining everything from home furnishings to automobiles to electric shavers and hair dryers.

America's music was changing, too. The Big Band Era was drawing to a close. People were dancing and romancing to the sound of smaller combos. Bands became streamlined along with everything else—

geared to the brisk pace of modernity. This new American music and lifestyle called for a new breed of musical instruments. That call was answered by a man from Fullerton, California, named Clarence Leo Fender, a post-war entrepreneur and inventor in the classic mold. He started the Fender Electric Instrument Company in 1946.

Rather than following centuries of European tradition, Fender created brand-new designs for a brand-new era. One huge innovation was that the guitars' necks were bolted to their simple, solid slab bodies, rather than joined and glued in as luthiers had been doing for hundreds of years. This was conducive to mass production, but also made for ease of repair. Fender brought the idea of modularity to guitar design—interchangeable parts—a development that would spark a passion for hot-rodding guitars in later decades.

Introduced in 1949, the Fender Telecaster (originally called the Broadcaster) is a masterpiece of functionality: a practical, affordable tool for the working musician, a fine instrument in every respect. Introduced in 1954, the Fender Stratocaster is even more: a thing of beauty, a masterpiece of American design that ranks right up there with the Empire State Building and the '57 Chevy. The sound of Fender guitars was as new and exciting as their look—a clean, clear, sparkling tone, as inviting as a crystal blue swimming pool on a hot summer day. Soon players from every musical walk of life—from singing cowboys to lounge smoothies—were flocking to Fender instruments and amps.

Playboy of the Western World

Good-timing, high-rolling Bob Wills was the ideal figurehead for the style that came to be known as western swing. Wills drew upon all the types of music that could be heard around his native Texas during his formative years—bluegrass, blues, jazz, mariachi, swing, and Tin Pan Alley pop—imparting a dash of urban sophistication to old-time fiddle music. Formed in 1933, Wills' Texas Playboys were one of the first bands to incorporate electric string instruments into their music. Initially loathed by the country music establishment in Nashville, electric instruments were brought onto the stage of the Grand Ole Opry, and into the hearts of country and western lovers, by Bob Wills and his Texas Playboys.

In 1943 Wills and his band moved from Oklahoma to California, where many of their Texan and Okie fans had found work in the wartime defense industry. Shortly thereafter Bob struck up a relationship with Leo Fender and his then-brand-new company. Bob Wills and his Texas Playboys were the first big-name band to get behind Fender instruments. Ol' Bob was rarely seen without his trademark Stetson hat, a big cigar, his fiddle, and some great Fender gear, like the rare old Pro amp he's plugged into at this late-'40s gig.

"Take It Away, Leon!"

When listeners heard Bob Wills let go with that famous exclamation, they knew they were in for some rip-roaring steel guitar playing. Leon McAuliffe was still in his teens when he joined up with Bob Wills in the early 1930s. Guitar amplification was a brand-new notion back then, but when McAuliffe suggested that it might be good to amplify his steel guitar, Wills readily accepted the idea. When the Texas Playboys were signed to the American Recording Company in the mid '30s, Wills worked hard to persuade the label to record McAuliffe's "Steel Guitar Rag," which quickly became a classic and a vehicle for McAuliffe's own notoriety. Leon left the Texas Playboys in 1942. Remaining in Oklahoma, he put his own band together. Like Wills, he became closely involved with Fender during the '40s. From then on, he remained a frequent visitor to the Fender plant, an advisor, endorsee, and friend up to the time of his death, at age 71, in 1988. Here Leon is seen fronting his band with a Fender Dual 8 Professional steel guitar.

"TAKE IT AWA"

"LEON"

Leo at Work

While he wasn't a musician himself, Leo Fender worked closely with many musicians in the development of his instruments. Here Leo (far right) is seen at the Fender factory with (left to right) Dub Williams and Eddie Miller—composers of country-pop crossover standard "Release Me"—and employee Lydia Sanchez, during the winter of 1950–51. Miller was one of many guitarists who worked at the Fender factory in the early days. In fact, he wrote the lyric for "Release Me" in the Fender restroom. The song has been covered by over 400 artists and was a big hit for Engelbert Humperdinck in the '70s. Miller was a lucky guy. The Fender facility only acquired restrooms in 1950. Before that, employees had to go across the street to the railroad station.

The Final Prototype

Leo Fender and his assistant George Fullerton built several prototypes of the instrument that was to become the Fender Telecaster. It was Leo's policy to place prototype guitars in the hands of working musicians for them to "field test" at gigs. This photo shows the final prototype built for the Telecaster before the instrument went into production in 1949. It was given to local guitarist Roy Watkins (right), who was "Jimmy" in the duo "Ted and Jimmy." The reason why Roy was called "Jimmy" onstage has been lost to history. The Telecaster itself went through some confusing name changes too. Initially called the Broadcaster, its name was changed to Telecaster to avoid a potential conflict with the Gretsch company, which manufactured a series of drums called Broadkaster. While the name change was in the works, Fender issued a few guitars with no name on the headstock. Some wag branded these guitars "Nocasters," and the name has stuck to these extremely rare and collectible curios ever since. Fender also manufactured a budget-line, single-pickup version of the Telecaster, which was called the Esquire. The prototype in the photo bears marked affinities to the Esquire as well.

14

Shamblin Man

Eldon Shamblin was another vital member of Bob Wills' Texas Playboys. The first known country musician to experiment with a solidbody electric Spanish guitar, Shamblin joined the Playboys in 1937. He contributed some brilliant arrangements to the band and co-authored the showcase "Twin Guitar Special" with Leon McAuliffe in 1941. In 1954 Eldon became the recipient of one of the first-ever Stratocasters. The Texas Playboys tour bus had pulled up to the Fender factory, as it usually did when the band hit town. Shamblin was shown a strange-looking new guitar and asked to field-test it. It's been his main guitar ever since.

The large photo shows Shamblin (right) at the Fender plant in 1957. Fender employee Earl Finley (left) is stringing and adjusting Shamblin's Strat. Forrest White, then the Fender plant manager, is standing next to Shamblin.

(Inset:) Eldon and his '54 Strat are in fine shape in this 1988 snapshot. With the exception of removing the tremolo arm, he has kept the gold-finished instrument in the same stock condition it was when Leo Fender first handed it to him in 1954 (note the volume and tone knobs). That's bassist and Playboys alumnus Joe Frank Ferguson in back.

15

The Mighty Wolf

It wasn't only country and western musicians who played Fender instruments in the early days. As this photo shows, the great bluesman Howlin' Wolf was a Fender man too. Born Chester Arthur Burnett on June 10, 1910, in West Point, Mississippi, the Wolf stood 6'3" when he grew to manhood. His weight has been placed at anywhere from 275 to 300 pounds. His powerful, unmistakable voice carried the ancient authority of a traditional African *griot* (a musical storyteller and keeper of the tribe's collective memory and folk wisdom). But for all its gruffness, it's a voice filled with humor, joy, and the easy rhythm of a born raconteur. Howlin' Wolf cut his first sides in 1948 at Sam Phillips' studio in Memphis. By 1952 he'd begun his lifelong relationship with Chess Records and became one of the definitive artists of the

Chicago blues style. The Howlin' Wolf persona was delineated by Burnett's own compositions and the songs penned for him by Willie Dixon—blues masterpieces like "The Red Rooster," "300 Pounds of Joy," "Evil," and "Down in the Bottom." The Wolf's trademark howl was punctuated by his own able guitar and harmonica playing and also the guitar work of the sublime Hubert Sumlin. In the '60s Howlin' Wolf became the idol of English rockers like the Rolling Stones and Eric Clapton, with whom he recorded the memorable *London Howlin' Wolf Sessions* in 1971. When he died on January 10, 1976, one of the most distinctive voices of this century was silenced—but not lost. His records will be treasured for as long as people are born with two ears and a soul.

Fender on TV

It's no accident that the Telecaster was named with the same prefix as that other ground-breaking entertainment innovation of the late '40s and early '50s. The burgeoning new medium of television provided important early exposure for Fender instruments and the people who played them. The "City at Night" program, broadcast over Hollywood's KTLA-TV, even visited the Fender factory in 1956. So it's no surprise that many of the endorsees who appeared in early Fender catalogs were artists known to the public mainly through that magical new medium of the post-war world.

(Photos, top to bottom:) Comedian Red Skelton had his own program and apparently didn't mind posing with a nice looking guitar. Extravagant pianist Liberace was a favorite of early TV audiences and gave his bassist, Bob Manners, a boost by appearing with him in the '56 Fender catalog. Buddy Merrill was Lawrence Welk's guitarist. Alvino Rey's orchestra often backed the King Sisters, and the virtuosic Rey delighted novelty-happy '50s TV audiences with his "talking" Fender pedal steel guitar. Speaking of novelties, Jerry Murad's Harmonicats were frequent guests on Ed Sullivan's program and other early variety shows, tooting reed instruments great and small through Fender amps. And from the mid '50s well into the '60s, it just wouldn't be a Fender catalog without the Mary Kaye Trio.

the dawn of the rock era
1956-60

An unexpected but exuberant wedding took place during the mid '50s down in the sultry American South. Rhythm and Blues tied the knot with Country and Western. One family traced its roots back to Africa, the other to Europe. Their firstborn was named rock and roll.

At first, the world was shocked. But after a while, the whole world rocked.

This bold new sound called for bold new instruments—ones that broke with tradition in a stylish, confident way. So it's no surprise that Fender guitars and amps played a big part in the birth of rock and roll. This era witnessed some blessed events at the Fender factory, too. The Musicmaster and Duo-Sonic arrived in '56 and the sleek, chic Jazzmaster came into the world in 1958. Fender and Rock: another harmonious couple, still together today.

The Voice that Rocked the World

Although Fender amps are best known for the way they complement the sound of electric guitars and basses, here we see the King of Rock and Roll, Elvis Aron Presley, using a Fender Bandmaster for a vocal amp during an appearance at the 1955 Tupelo County Fair. But wait, isn't that Phil Silvers—in his TV role as "Sergeant Bilko"—behind the piano?

19

Blue Gene Bops

An ex-sailor from Virginia, Gene Vincent (born Eugene Vincent Craddock) didn't let a bad left leg stop

him from bopping to the top of the charts with the 1956 hit "Be-Bop-A-Lula." Vincent and his band,

the Blue Caps, were the first rock and roll group to become official Fender endorsers.

51- 20

Hey, Jayne, Let's See You Do This!

Hitting the big screen in 1956, *The Girl Can't Help It* was a breakthrough film in introducing rock and roll to mass audiences and erasing the "color line" in popular music. In a pivotal scene, blonde bombshell actress Jayne Mansfield endeavors to catch the eye of a swanky nightclub audience while the house band—played by Little Richard and his group, the Upsetters—pounds out a furious rendition of their tune "She's Got It." Even the surrealistically endowed Ms. Mansfield had her work cut out for her trying to upstage rock and roll's most flamboyant wild man. This famous promo still encapsulates the moment: Richard gets a leg up on the situation while guitarist Nathaniel Douglas provides moral support on a sweet Telecaster-and-Bassman combination.

21

Buddy Makes It Big

Buddy Holly had it all: the voice, the songs, the boy-next-door looks, and the chug-a-lug Stratocaster guitar style. Buddy's tune "That'll Be the Day" topped the charts in 1957, followed in short order by "Peggy Sue." Here Buddy is seen with his band, the Crickets, on a *très moderne* late-'50s TV set. Holly's death in a plane crash in 1959—an accident that also claimed the lives of Ritchie Valens and the Big Bopper—saddened rock and roll fans everywhere. Buddy left his stamp on many later rock-and-rollers, including the Beatles, whose vocal style and "insect novelty" name were inspired by the "Chirping Crickets."

"And this, Gentlemen, Is What They Call a Lick"

Jerry Lee Lewis (seated), Don Everly (one half of the Everly Brothers—holding microphone), and Jimmy Velvet can't take their eyes off the capoed fretboard of Buddy Holly's Stratocaster in this rare photo. Jimmy Velvet—a former member of Elvis Presley's entourage and currently president of the Elvis Presley Museum—provided this shot of a classic rock and roll moment.

The Man in Black Steps into the Spotlight

Guitarist Luther Perkins (right) backed Johnny Cash as a member of the Tennessee Two (along with bassist Marshall Grant) starting with Cash's earliest sides for Sun Records in 1955. His distinctive style helped define the country side of the Sun Records sound on Cash hits like "Folsom Prison Blues" and "I Walk the Line." Here he plays a Jazzmaster while a Telecaster waits behind his Concert amp.

(Inset:) Sporting a supercool pair of two-tone shoes, Luther checks out an even cooler gold Jazzmaster and prototype Vibrasonic amp at the Fender plant in 1959. Fender employee Bob Hines looks on.

Ritchie Valens and His Strat

Los Angeles teenager Richard Valenzuela combined rock and roll with his own Mexican-American musical heritage to create the 1958 hits "La Bamba," "Come On, Let's Go," and "Donna." The world knew him—all too briefly—as Ritchie Valens. The 17-year-old Valens was one of the casualties in the 1959 plane crash that also took the lives of Buddy Holly and the Big Bopper. Valens' eternally youthful songs have lived on, in hit revivals by everyone from the McCoys to Los Lobos.

Father of the Electric Blues

McKinley Morganfield—better known as Muddy Waters—swapped his acoustic guitar for a Telecaster and forged the raw, compelling style the world now calls Chicago blues. Muddy's electric slide playing—generally executed on a late-'50s red Tele and Fender Super amp—was also immensely influential on rock and rollers like the Rolling Stones, who took their name from one of his songs.

Photographer Terry Cryer caught this shot of Muddy backstage at the Marquee Club in London in 1958.

The Moonglows Croon

Doo-wop stylists the Moonglows pose with a Telecaster in this suave promo shot. The Moonglows were one of the important vocal harmony groups to emerge from the area around Washington, D.C., during the '50s. They played a vital role in creating the doo-wop sound and also had an influence on the development of Motown. Marvin Gaye sang with the Moonglows early on. Lead singer Harvey Fuqua is seen at the far right in this photo.

Master of the Telecaster

You can hear all the essentials of Albert Collins' incisive blues guitar style on his very first single, "The Freeze" b/w "Collins Shuffle" (1958). Inspired by Clarence "Gatemouth" Brown, Collins bought his first Fender—an Esquire—in 1952. From there he moved on to the Telecasters that were to become his lifelong trademark. His unmistakable style revolved around an open F-minor tuning, his use of a capo high on the fretboard (usually around the seventh or eighth fret), and his use of bare fingers rather than a plectrum to pick the strings.

The Effervescent
Speedy West

Playing a Fender Model 1000 pedal steel made specially for him, Fender endorser Speedy West leads an all-Fender band through a set in a shed somewhere in '50s America.

the early '60s

The first years of the '60s saw an explosion of pop styles across the U.S.A.—surfing sounds from sunny California, Brill Building song hits from the concrete canyons of New York, the Motown groove out of Detroit, and everything in between. Then, in the frozen February of 1964, four lads from Liverpool appeared on "The Ed Sullivan Show." The Beatles had arrived. The British Invasion that swept America and the world was a cultural phenomenon of unprecedented proportions.

It was a friendly invasion. The young English musicians who landed in the States turned out to have a deep love of American blues, rock, pop, folk, and country sounds. Soon musical ideas and influences were flowing in both directions, back and forth across the Atlantic.

As pop music grew and diversified during the fertile early '60s, so did Fender. The company increased its staff and facilities to meet the brisk new demand for Fender instruments both at home and abroad. The product line expanded to include acoustic guitars, electric pianos, and more amplifiers and electric guitars than they'd ever made before. This was the era when classic Fender guitars like the Jaguar and Mustang made their debuts.

The self-contained guitar group came into its own during these fast-paced years. In garages and basements everywhere, young players were getting together to see if they could wring fame and fortune from a backbeat and some chiming guitar chords.

"DICK DALE" & DEL-TONES

The King of Surf Guitar

Dick Dale and his Del-Tones rock it up on the set of a local TV dance party. A pioneer of the surf guitar style, Dale (at center stage in photo) is a left-handed guitarist who uses a conventional right-handed stringing on his lefty Strat. Dale's tireless demands for bigger and louder amplifiers during the early '60s contributed to the development of the Showman and Dual Showman amplifiers.

29

Annette Meets the Beach Boys

From the moment their 1963 hit "Surfin' U.S.A." broke onto the charts, the Beach Boys came to personify the California youth experience—surfboards, hot rods, and, of course, Fender guitars, which they endorsed for years. Here they're seen with the Queen of Beach Movies, Annette Funicello, performing the title song to the 1965 Disney film *The Monkey's Uncle.*

Venturesome Duo

Starting with their 1960 hit "Walk, Don't Run," the Ventures featured that sparkly, clean Fender sound in recordings that helped define the surf instrumental genre. While their records evoked the fun and sun of California's Pacific coastline, the Ventures were actually from Tacoma, Washington. Pictured are Ventures guitarists Don Wilson (with Stratocaster) and Bob Bogle (with Jazzmaster).

The Shadows Know

Led by bespectacled guitarist Hank Marvin, the Shadows were Britain's most successful instrumental group during the early '60s, known worldwide for their 1960 hit "Apache." The Shadows did much to popularize Fender instruments in the U.K. and were a huge influence on many guitarists of the British Invasion, including George Harrison and Pete Townshend. The group also inspired a boy named Mark Knopfler to start playing guitar. He eventually made his main axe a red Strat like Marvin's. In 1992 Fender brought out a special Hank Marvin model.

Buck Owens and Don Rich

Although he was born in Sherman, Texas, Alvis Edgar "Buck" Owens (right, with Tele) put the California town of Bakersfield on the country music map during the early '60s. It was there that he started the Buckaroos, appointing his good friend Don Rich (left, with Tele) the band's lead guitarist and musical director. Owens' plaintive, homespun vocals and solid Telecaster rhythms found their ideal complement in Rich's twangy Tele leads and high, lonesome vocal harmonies. Rich's untimely death in a motorcycle accident in 1974 put an end to the Buckaroos' special chemistry, but their Bakersfield sound lives on in modern-day artists like Dwight Yoakam.

33

Motortown Revue

Brainchild of Motown Records chief Berry Gordy, the first Motortown Revue kicked off on November 2, 1962, at the Boston Arena. The traveling roadshow was a major success, despite a grueling schedule that had 45 singers and musicians all riding one big bus and playing 19 cities in 23 days. When the Revue reached its final destination—a celebratory nine nights at the Apollo Theater in Harlem—a new American musical empire had been established.

Here the very debutante-looking Supremes strike a harmonious pose. Motown's mighty Robert White is on a Fender Jazzmaster (left).

James Jamerson Anchors the Motown Sound

The elegant economy and rhythmic savvy of James Jamerson's bass style were the foundation of innumerable Motown hits. Here he's seen in 1965 at the Blues Unlimited club in Detroit, playing his 1962 P-Bass.

(Inset:) Jamerson's formidable skills as a session man were honed by miles and miles of roadwork during the early '60s. Here he's center stage, behind the great R&B singer and showman Jackie Wilson at a 1961 gig in Milford, Delaware.

The Wrecking Crew in Action

Ace producer Phil Spector, "the First Tycoon of Teen," recruited Hollywood's coolest and craziest players for his studio band. Crammed into a tiny studio at Gold Star Recording, Spector's "Wrecking Crew" built the massive Wall of Sound heard on hit singles by the Ronettes, Crystals, Righteous Brothers, and others. Glen Campbell, Leon Russell, and Larry Knechtel were among the noted musicians who made up the Crew's ever-fluctuating membership. Though they were initially Spector's band, many Wrecking Crew alumni also played on classic sides by the Beach Boys, Byrds, Mamas and Papas, Sonny and Cher, and just about anyone else who made a hit record in Los Angeles during the early to mid '60s.

Here's the Wrecking Crew on a '63 date. (Clockwise from bottom left:) Al Delory on keyboards, Carol Kaye (shades and Fender Jazzmaster), Bill Pitman, Tommy Tedesco, unknown guitarist, Roy Caton (trumpet), Jay Migliori (trumpet), Hal Blaine (drums), Steve Douglas (tenor sax), unknown child, and Ray Pohlman (Fender Precision Bass).

The Godfather Takes Control

"The Godfather of Soul," "The Hardest-Working Man in Show Business," James Brown is known to be a notoriously demanding band leader. In this 1964 promo shot, Smash Records decided to portray Brown in his element, leading his Fender-equipped band through a new arrangement. The mid '60s were a particularly fertile period for Brown, a time that saw him breaking through to a larger audience than ever with hits like "I Got You (I Feel Good)" and "Papa's Got a Brand New Bag."

37

Original Ravers

A rarely seen outtake from the '65 photo session for *Having a Rave-Up with the Yardbirds*, one of the most influential guitar records of the mid '60s. Jeff Beck's "most blueswailing" Esquire excursions helped set the vogue for extended guitar solos in rock, heralding the transition from British Invasion pop to the psychedelic era.

Rhythm guitarist Chris Dreja strums a Jaguar at left, while a very youthful Jeff Beck frets an Esquire at right. The Yardbirds were the group that also brought Eric Clapton and Jimmy Page to prominence.

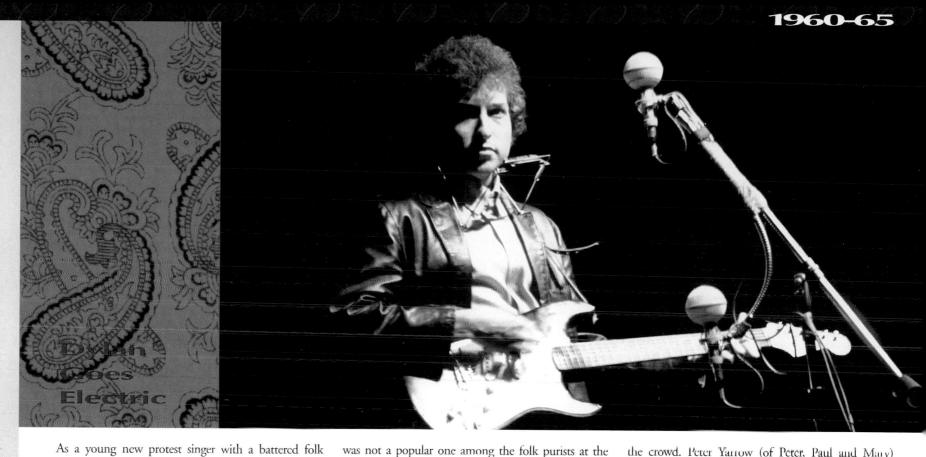

Dylan Goes Electric

As a young new protest singer with a battered folk guitar and a head full of eloquent songs, Bob Dylan had been the toast of the Newport Folk Festival in 1963 and '64. He received quite a different reception on the afternoon of July 25, 1965, when he walked onto the Newport stage sporting a sunburst Stratocaster and black leather jacket. Dylan's decision to combine the electrified beat of rock and roll with his early folk style

was not a popular one among the folk purists at the festival. The sight of an electric guitar on the Newport stage seemed to them an outright sacrilege. Backed by the Paul Butterfield Blues Band, Dylan got through three songs before the crowd began to heckle him openly. "Get rid of that guitar!" someone yelled. "Go back to 'The Ed Sullivan Show'," jeered another voice. Dylan quit the stage as derisive laughter swelled from

the crowd. Peter Yarrow (of Peter, Paul and Mary) pleaded for a round of applause to bring the singer back onstage. When Dylan finally returned to the platform, he had tears in his eyes and his old acoustic guitar in his hands. He faced the hostile audience and sang, "It's All over Now, Baby Blue."

But a whole new thing was just beginning.

the late
'60s

Vietnam, the Summer of Love, Black Power, Kent State, Woodstock,... In the late '60s, popular music became a force for social change—the voice of a newly empowered youth culture. Pop music intensified in every way. Volume levels increased dramatically. Textures deepened. So did the lyrics. Song lengths went far beyond the traditional three-and-a-half-minute limit. New musical styles emerged—psychedelia, soul, folk rock. Many of these styles were based on the unique musical patterns and sonic properties that could be coaxed from a greatly amplified, electronically processed electric guitar. Jimi Hendrix prophesied (not quite accurately) that we'd never hear surf music again. We'd certainly never hear it in quite the same way—not after our ears had been "experienced" by Hendrix and his contemporaries.

The times were a-changin' for Fender, too. In January of 1965 the company was purchased by CBS Inc. for $13 million. It was an unprecedentedly high figure for the time. But Fender's new owners had acquired a valuable asset. Demand for Fender instruments mushroomed. Guitarists like Pete Townshend and Jimi Hendrix sparked a fresh wave of Strat-mania. Meanwhile, Fender continued to press forward. Nineteen sixty-five also saw the introduction of the stylish Fender Electric XII. Players in every style were searching for new sounds. Fender had what they wanted.

Hendrix Plays Monterey

Held on June 16–18, 1967, in Monterey, California, the First International Pop Festival was the crystallizing event of the psychedelic era. It also marked the American debut of the Jimi Hendrix Experience. No one in the audience was quite prepared for the otherworldly sounds this bold young guitarist could wrest from his Stratocaster or the reckless passion of his performance. At the climax of his set, Hendrix flung his Strat to the stage, straddled the prone instrument, saturated it with lighter fluid, and set it ablaze. In a flash, Jimi had become a legend and the Strat had entered the realms of rock mythology.

41

Bob Dylan
plays

Album of Stars

By the late '60s, Fender's endorsement program had grown to include major artists in virtually every musical genre—and, well, a few not-so-major artists, too. In addition to its regular catalogs, the company began publishing the *Fender Album of Stars* series, portfolios filled with artist photos suitable for framing, culled from Fender's vast and variegated family of players. (From upper left:) Jazz bassist Monk Montgomery and his brother, guitar legend Wes; psychedelic rockers the Peanut Butter Conspiracy; Bob Dylan; Wayne Newton (en route to Vegas); blues harp master James Cotton and his band; the First Edition (yes, that's Kenny Rogers with that Coronado bass and wild striped pants); Rick Nelson and his long-time lead guitarist James Burton; and Jimi Hendrix.

the late '60s

Look Ma, I'm a Bass Player!

Bob Dylan cracks a smile in this rarely seen outtake from his *Fender Album of Stars* photo session.

Architects of the Stax Sound

Booker T. and the MGs did double duty as recording artists in their own right and backing band for the Stax label's prodigious talent roster. Steve Cropper's crisp Tele style and the percussive pulse of Donald "Duck" Dunn's P-Bass energized many a hit by Otis Redding, Sam and Dave, Wilson Pickett, and other Stax giants. With Booker T. Jones on organ and Al Jackson on drums, the MGs were an unbeatable team.

Pete Takes Twelve

Few players did more than Pete Townshend to revolutionize the nature of rock guitar in the late 1960s. He developed an intensely rhythmic style—rhythmic to the point of violence. Spurred by an interest in avant garde music, Pete was the first guitarist to realize the full expressive potential of the "accidental" noises an electric guitar could make—feedback, the percussive crackle of toggle switches, the screech of strings being scraped with a mike stand, and, ultimately, the din of the instrument being smashed to splinters on a concert stage. This welter of aggression was offset by the melodious, ringing electric 12-string style of early Who singles. Townshend's explosive guitar work and inventive, narrative songwriting helped make the Who one of the most exciting live acts of the late '60s. Jimi Hendrix was among the many guitarists influenced by Townshend, even emulating the latter's choice of equipment. Pete mainly played Strats onstage during this era, but here he's seen in the studio strumming a Fender Electric XII.

45

Funk Forebear

Larry Graham's pioneering bass work with Sly and the Family Stone established many of the grooves and techniques that would form the basis of funk bass playing in the '70s. Bass moved into the foreground of pop music arrangements once Graham began popping and slapping his strings, showing how the instrument could be used for percussive treble accentuations while also holding down the bottom. Here he's seen playing a Jazz Bass at a Family Stone rehearsal; that's Sly Stone on drums.

From Yardbirds to Led Zep... a Turn of the Page

Jimmy Page was the last of the great guitarists to play with the Yardbirds, following in the wake of Eric Clapton and Jeff Beck. (Beck and Page actually performed together in the band for a brief while.) During the final phases of the Yardbirds, Page laid the groundwork for much of what was to become Led Zeppelin—a band he formed in 1968, soon after the Yardbirds split up. Page was playing Telecasters extensively during this period, and his Tele had a role in creating the heavy guitar sound of the first Led Zeppelin album. Here he's caught in action with the Yardbirds at the Anderson Theater in New York City.

Elvis' Fender Army

Elvis Presley is flanked by a phalanx of Fender flailers in this number from his 1968 film *Speedway*. The movie, which co-starred Nancy Sinatra, was hardly the King's brightest cinematic moment. But this still is pretty groovy, and Elvis at this point was just months away from his triumphant live "comeback" TV special.

the late '60s

David Gilmour Discovers the Strat

By the late '60s Pink Floyd had weathered the mental collapse of their first leader, the brilliant Syd Barrett, and solidified their reputation as fabricators of mesmerizing aural soundscapes both live and in the studio.

Guitarist David Gilmour was Barrett's replacement. Like Syd, he originally played a Telecaster—an instrument he received as a gift on his 21st birthday. But in the summer of 1968, Gilmour's birthday present was lost as the band was traveling to begin its very first American tour. He decided to replace the instrument with a Stratocaster, and has since become closely associated with Strats. Included in his vast guitar collection, in fact, is a Stratocaster bearing serial number 001!

Here Gilmour (left) is seen in concert in 1969 with the classic Pink Floyd lineup: drummer Nick Mason, keyboardist Rick Wright, and bassist Roger Waters.

Woodstock

Approximately 400,000 people converged on Max Yasgur's farm in upstate New York between August 16 and 18th,1969, for what was billed as "3 days of peace & music." The Woodstock Festival marked hippiedom's transition from an underground scene to a phenomenon of mass culture. Jimi Hendrix's performance encapsulated the rapid changes that had taken place in music in the two short years since his band had made its American debut at Monterey Pop. With the Experience recently disbanded, Jimi was just finding his way into a new musical context that included elements of third-world percussion and free jazz restlessness. He closed his set—and the entire Woodstock festival—with a chilling solo guitar performance of "The Star-Spangled Banner," recreating the sounds of strafing jet fighters and exploding artillery on his Fender Stratocaster. In so vividly evoking the horrors of war within the harmonic cadences of his country's national anthem, Hendrix offered a critique of the still-raging Vietnam war—a statement perhaps more eloquent than any political speech. The fact that nearly half a million kids had come together amid mud, rain, and chaos without a single violent incident seemed a harbinger of a better world. The dream, unfortunately, proved as tragically short-lived as Jimi Hendrix himself.

An Okie from Muskogee

The late '60s weren't all free love and anti-Vietnam sentiment. In 1969 Merle Haggard crossed over from country audiences to the mainstream with "Okie from Muskogee," whose lyrics denounced the hippie counterculture and celebrated the virtues of being drug-free, clean-cut, and patriotic. The song sparked lots of debate, including speculation as to how far Haggard had his tongue planted in his cheek when he wrote the arch-conservative lyric. Not quite the ideal poster boy for law-abiding citizenhood, ol' Merle got to witness Johnny Cash's historic first free concert at Folsom Prison in 1958—as a compulsory guest of the State. Here Merle stands at attention with his Telecaster at the WSM 42nd Anniversary celebration for the Grand Ole Opry.

50

Farewell Beatles

No event symbolized the end of the '60s more poignantly than the breakup of the Beatles. The film *Let It Be* documented the band's recording sessions for their album of the same name, culminating in what proved to be their final live performance—up on the roof of Abbey Road studios in London. The rosewood Telecaster that George Harrison is seen playing throughout the film was presented to the Beatles by Fender, as a result of conversations between John, Paul, and Fender exec Don Randall in 1969. The company also provided the Fender Rhodes electric piano played by Billy Preston for the album and film. Lennon and Harrison also traded off on a Fender Bass VI to hold down the low end when McCartney played piano. Rock was changed forever by the four young men who played their last public notes together on that cold London rooftop in January of 1969. The continuing popularity of their music has shown that the Beatles weren't just for the '60s, but for all time.

the '70s

Pop music spread in many directions during the '70s, as the late-'60s counterculture was gradually absorbed into the mainstream. The riff-oriented rock pioneered by groups like Cream and the Jimi Hendrix Experience transformed into heavy metal, progressive rock, and fusion. Sixties free radio became the album rock format. Free love reemerged as disco hedonism and the festive androgyny of glam rock. Soul music got psychedelicized and became funk. The hippie blues boom went back to its roots and became southern boogie. The Partridge Family took over from the Monkees as the reigning pop act on TV. Folk rock split off into country rock and the '70s singer/songwriter boom.

But as many rockers scrambled to go country in the '70s, many country artists opted for the uptown sophistication of the "countrypolitan" sound. Meanwhile, a crucial new rhythm called reggae came up from Jamaica like a tropical storm, influencing everyone from Paul Simon to the Clash.

Rock and roll grew to adulthood in the '70s. For some, it had become a little too mature. By the end of the decade, punk rock had issued its belligerent challenge to the status quo. The revolution wasn't televised, but it was Telecastered: Many of the snarling young hellions of the new rock came to the fray clutching Fender guitars. The Stratocaster celebrated its 25th anniversary in 1979. But no one called it a dinosaur.

Quintessential Rock-and-Roller

The early '70s were a creative high point for the Rolling Stones. They were in top form as a live band and turning out studio gems on the order of *Sticky Fingers* and *Exile on Main Street*. It was around this time that Keith Richards switched to old Teles and Esquires as his stage guitars of choice.

Richards, Mick Jagger, and Brian Jones started the Rolling Stones in January 1962, based on a shared passion for American blues and R&B. Richards' guitar work has always exhibited a bluesman's sense of economy and emotional directness. A supple rhythm player, he's also the author of some of the most memorable Stones guitar licks. His flair for big chordal hooks ("Jumpin' Jack Flash," "Street Fighting Man," "Start Me Up") is one of the foundations on which rock itself rests. With his unique five-string open-G tuning and inimitable swagger, Richards has instigated many a classic Stones moment.

53

the '70s

Metal Main Man

Ritchie Blackmore's incendiary Strat style blazed the trail for heavy metal in the early '70s on Deep Purple albums like *In Rock*, *Fireball*, and *Machine Head*. Blackmore is the author of what is probably the most-played riff in all rock guitar: the four-bar, blues-based figure that sets up the verses to "Smoke on the Water." Ritchie left Deep Purple in 1974 and formed the highly successful group Rainbow.

Studio Creature

A distinguished alumnus of Phil Spector's Wrecking Crew, Carol Kaye has maintained an active career as a first-call session ace. Here she lays down a relaxed P-Bass groove for a Hampton Hawes record during a 1974 session at Fantasy Studios in Berkeley, California. Not only a consummate bass guitar stylist, Carol also really knew how to accessorize for that ultra-'70s "red carpet" studio decor.

On the Job with "The Boss"

Bruce Springsteen's ability to extract heartfelt poetry from the American blue-collar experience gave rock and roll a unique new voice in the mid '70s. He became a major star in 1974 with the anthemic *Born to Run* and rock critic Jon Landau's prophetic declaration, "I have seen the future of rock and roll, and its name is Bruce Springsteen." Fittingly enough, Bruce chose a real workingman's guitar—a natural finish Esquire — as his axe. The instrument has become an icon in its own right, having graced hundreds of magazine covers down through the years.

55

Slowhand and Blackie

As he entered the second decade of his career, Eric Clapton moved away from the blues virtuosity of his early work with the Yardbirds, John Mayall's Bluesbreakers, and Cream. He embraced a more laid-back aesthetic and began working with American musicians down in the deep South, assembling what would become Derek and the Dominos.

Despite a tangle of personal problems, the '70s were a period of great commercial notoriety for Clapton. The phenomenal success of Derek and the Dominos' "Layla" was followed by Clapton's solo hit recording of Bob Marley's "I Shot the Sheriff" and FM radio staples like "Lay Down Sally" and "Wonderful Tonight."

Clapton first became interested in Stratocasters right at the dawn of the '70s—initially through Steve Winwood, who was in Blind Faith with Clapton and who used a Strat in that band. But it was down in Nashville in 1970 that Clapton wandered into a music store and got an irresistible deal on six old Strats. He gave one each to George Harrison, Pete Townshend, and Winwood. Of the three Strats he kept for himself, he took the parts he liked best and assembled the guitar the world knows as "Blackie." Named for its body color, "Blackie" is technically a mongrel. But its close association with Clapton has made it one of the most revered instruments in guitardom's noble peerage.

Roy Buchanan

The late Roy Buchanan didn't just play electric guitar; he played Telecaster. Along with guitarists like Danny Gatton, James Burton, and Jerry Donahue, Buchanan belonged to that elite cadre of players who have harvested the unique sonic qualities of the Telecaster to create highly original styles. From his self-titled debut album in 1972 onward, Buchanan's personal touch was unmistakable: soul searing top-string leads and a masterful command of harmonics. Here Roy is seen with his favorite Tele, "Nancy," onstage at the Roxy Theater in L.A.

The King's Man

To date, James Burton is the only guitarist who has worked with both Elvises (Presley and Costello). Burton created the signature lick on Dale Hawkins' "Susie-Q" and played on Ricky Nelson's string of hits in the late '50s and early '60s before accepting Elvis Presley's offer to come play guitar in his band in 1968. Burton was Presley's guitarist until the King's death, in 1977.

Burton is noted for his use of ultra-thin banjo strings on a Fender Telecaster, a combination that enables him to create distinctive, pedal-steel-like bent note licks. Here he is pictured with his signature paisley Telecaster.

That's no Elvis impersonator alongside Burton in this concert snapshot taken by an adoring fan at Madison Square Garden in 1973; that's the real Elvis. With those big white elephant bells sweeping around the stage, James probably never had to dust off his stomp boxes after a gig.

59

the '70s

The Ox Steps Forward

Always a fiercely assertive player, John Entwistle really brought his bass guitar to the forefront of the Who's music in the early '70s. His muted plectrum style on earlier Who records gave way to the exceedingly nimble five-finger right-hand work heard on tracks like "The Real Me," from *Quadrophenia* (1973). Solid yet agile, Entwistle always had just the right blend of melodicism and moxie to play alongside Pete Townshend. "I forced the bass to become a lead instrument," Entwistle recollects. "I used to get angry when I was called a bass player. As far as I was concerned, I was the lead guitarist, but I was doing it an octave lower. That seemed to work with the Who because Pete was very chord oriented."

Jaco Goes for the Top Notes

The dazzling bass virtuosity of Jaco Pastorius set a new standard for bass soloing and helped spearhead the jazz-rock fusion movement of the early and mid '70s. Jaco's *tour de force* fretless bass work on Weather Report's 1976 album *Black Market* helped the group break through to a wider audience. In his all-too-brief life, Jaco worked with many fusion-era greats, including Al Di Meola, Herbie Hancock, Pat Metheny, and Tom Scott. Joni Mitchell also tapped Jaco's vast talents for a number of her albums in the '70s, including *Mingus* (1979). Here Jaco is seen with his Fender Jazz Bass, a favorite instrument of his.

Beck Gets Wired

Having made some of the definitive rock guitar records of the '60s, Jeff Beck turned toward fusion during the '70s. It proved to be a great move, both artistically and commercially. Beck's 1975 opus *Blow by Blow* and the '76 masterpiece *Wired* are among the best-selling guitar instrumental records of all time. Fusion seemed to give Beck a canvas wide enough to accommodate his gravity-defying sense of fretboard dynamics and highly individual finger-plucked tone. Whereas he played an Esquire on his classic sides with the Yardbirds, he'd switched to a Stratocaster by the time of *Wired*, as he showed the crowd during this 1977 appearance at the Starlite Amphitheater in Burbank. He has stuck with Strats ever since.

Blues Summit

Robert Cray (left) and Albert Collins toured together extensively during the mid '70s. Collins, a veteran bluesman (see "The Dawn of the Rock Era"), enjoyed a resurgence of popularity at this time. And Cray's own star was just rising—a bright new light in the blues firmament. Here the two are seen jamming at the San Francisco Blues Festival. Although Cray is best known for impassioned fretwork on his signature green Strat, he's seen here playing a Tele, while the late Collins fingerpicks his own well-known capoed Telecaster.

Two Legends Converge

In this 1976 photo, the late Frank Zappa holds one of his prized possessions: a guitar formerly owned by Jimi Hendrix and burned by Jimi at a 1968 gig in Miami. Zappa restored the guitar to playing condition, and it was later played by Steve Vai during his tenure in Zappa's band. One of our era's most significant composers, satirists, and guitar virtuosos, Zappa played Strats extensively during the latter part of his life and career.

Mommy, My Guitar Keeps Falling Off!

That nice sunburst Strat is no mere stage prop. Mick Jagger's role as the Rolling Stones' third guitarist has grown steadily over the years. Here we see him onstage at the Anaheim Stadium during the band's '78 tour.

65

Up from the Pubs

Dire Straits came out of England in 1978, playing a brand of roots rock enlivened by the dulcet tones of Mark Knopfler's Stratocaster. Knopfler's lyrical solos and ringing, stinging finger-picked sound are so instantly identifiable that many guitarists call the second notch on a five-position Strat switch "the Knopfler setting."

Post-Modern Guitar Hero

Like his friend Patti Smith, Tom Verlaine had a passion for French Symbolist poetry and Fender guitars. But while Smith focused mainly on the symbolic value of her Fender Duo-Sonic, Verlaine wrung sheer aural poetry from his Fender Jazzmaster.

A highly emotive, hallucinogenically intense stylist, Verlaine's dramatic finger vibrato and soaring string bends ushered in a new era of guitar playing. Born Tom Miller, Verlaine co-founded the band Television in 1974 with Richard Lloyd, whose searing Strat-craft provided the perfect tonal and melodic counterpoint to Verlaine's vocals and guitar. Television was one of the first rock bands to play at CBGB, the tiny New York Bowery bar where punk rock first coalesced—and where this gritty black-and-white shot of Tom with a customized Jazzmaster was taken. Television disbanded in 1978. (They reunited briefly for a recording and tour in 1992.) Their '77 debut album, *Marquee Moon*, is recognized as a landmark guitar record.

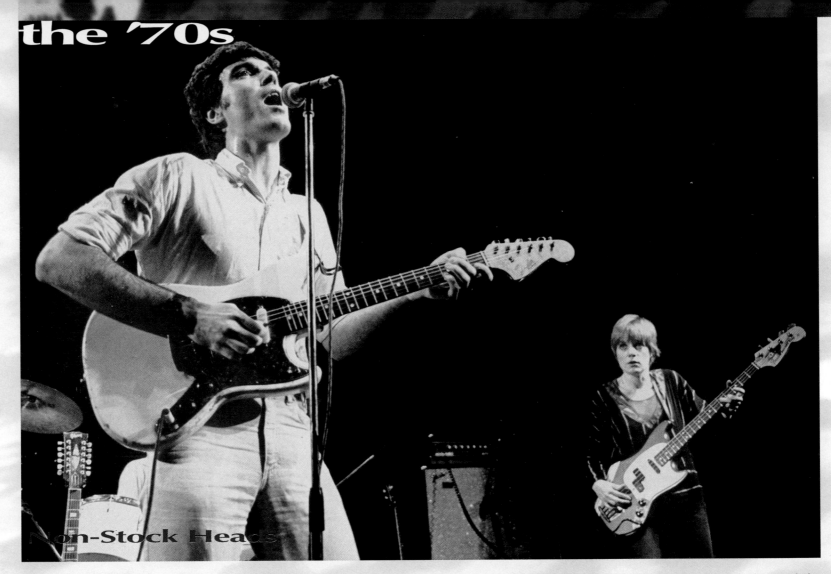

Non-Stock Heads

Along with Television and Patti Smith, the Talking Heads personified the more cerebral side of the punk scene that took shape around CBGB in the late '70s.

Early Talking Heads albums featured twitchy rhythms, bright, enigmatic lyrics, and a squeaky-clean, unmistakably Fender guitar sound. They became one of the most influential bands in modern rock. In the '80s, the group's lineup swelled and their musical vocabulary grew to include African polyrhythms and the experimental electronics of producer Brian Eno.

Here we see head Head David Byrne and bassist Tina Weymouth.

Sid's First Gig with the Pistols

Sid Vicious is the patron saint of punk nonmusicianship. A fanatically devoted rock fan, he got to live out the ultimate punter's fantasy: to climb up on stage and actually join his favorite band. Sid (John Ritchie) had followed the Sex Pistols ever since their first gigs around London. He was an old friend of Johnny Rotten's and part of the Pistols' inner circle. But when the band ousted their original bassist, Glen Matlock, for being too pop oriented, too musicianly, and too middle-class, Ritchie was elevated to the role of bass player. It was Rotten who christened him Sid Vicious. A complete fashion fetishist, Sid had the look, the attitude,…and absolutely not a clue about how to play bass. Rotten found this a refreshing change of pace from Matlock.

When Sid did his first gig with the Sex Pistols, at Notre Dame Hall in London in mid 1977, he'd never played bass guitar onstage with a group before. At the time of his death just a year and a half later, he was still a barely adequate bass player at best. But he sure looked cool wearing one. Sid embodied the punk ideal that playing rock isn't the privilege of a small musical elite, but something that anyone can do if they've got the passion and verve for it. That's why punk kids loved him and always will. Other bassists have explored the musical potentialities of the Fender Precision Bass; Sid showed what a great fashion accessory it could be.

Police Raid Madame Wong's

Though they came up on the punk/new wave circuit, the Police were actually made up of seasoned musicians whose sound drew on everything from reggae to progressive rock. Their spare, three-piece lineup gave each player maximum space in which to orchestrate the band's catchy, clever songs. Photographer Jeff Mayer caught the Police red-handed at late-'70s L.A. punk haunt Madame Wong's, a stop on their first-ever U.S. tour: A totally buffed-out Sting plucks a fretless P-Bass while Andy Summers strums a Tele and drummer Stewart Copeland wonders if blondes really do have more fun.

This Year's Model?

Like his stage name and Buddy Holly-style specs, Elvis Costello's choice of guitar reflected the singer/songwriter's deep fascination with American popular culture. Retro yet modern, the Fender Jazzmaster became part of the "new wave" aesthetic that gelled around performers like Costello (real name: Declan MacManus) during the late '70s. His aggressive, rhythmic use of the Jazzmaster on his early albums was perfectly suited to the propulsive, combo-organ-driven attack of his band, the Attractions. The "new Elvis" was one of the players who touched off a revival of interest in Jazzmasters and Jaguars—an interest that is still very much alive among today's alternative rock guitarists.

the early '80s

For pop music, the '80s started on August 1, 1981. That was the day MTV began. The video music boom ushered in a new era of visual style. And a new pantheon of video-friendly pop stars—Michael Jackson, Prince, Madonna,... The vibe was high-gloss and extremely fast-paced. For a brief period, it looked like the venerable electric guitar would be swept aside on a tide of synth pop and eyeliner.

This, of course, was not to be. Guitar turned out to be an essential tool for influential modern rock artists like U2, the Cure, the Police, and the Smiths, whose textural, orchestral use of the instrument opened up new vistas. And then there was something called

shred. Van Halen laid the foundations back in the late '70s—a stunning lexicon of fretboard tapping and lethal divebombing. By the early '80s these techniques had spawned an army of young guitarists who played with manic intensity, setting a new land speed record for the electric guitar. Many of these guitarists found mass acceptance in a new breed of metal bands that emerged in the '80s. Detractors called them "hair bands," or "metal lite," but groups like Quiet Riot, Bon Jovi, and Def Leppard came to be the dominant force on MTV as the decade reached its midpoint.

The '80s weren't all gloss and glamour, however. The hard urban realism of hip hop came on strong at this time. And there was a resurgence of interest in blues

and American roots music, as new artists like Robert Cray and Stevie Ray Vaughan came to the fore, and veteran bluesmen like Albert Collins and Buddy Guy found a responsive new audience.

Fender entered the '80s with an eye to the future, but also a growing appreciation of the past. They brought back the traditional Fender four-bolt neck joint and launched a large-scale modernization of the factory. The company was on the verge of a new era.

Symbol o' the Times

Few stars personify the '80s more thoroughly than the man born Prince Rodgers Nelson. His boundless talent lustfully embraced the decade's fascination with excess, hedonistic indulgence, and artifice for artifice's sake. A light-skinned, androgynous black man, Prince had the power to crash through the boundaries of race and sexual orientation and appeal to everyone. His 1980 breakthrough album *Dirty Mind* shocked a lot of people and shook up music biz marketing categories by combining elements of rock, funk, cabaret, and gospel—sexiness and spirituality—in one humongous love groove.

Prince was a staunch Telecaster player during this period and continues to employ Teles on recordings to this day. His polymorphous talents as singer, songwriter, director, actor, record producer, and multi-instrumentalist tend to obscure the fact that he is one wicked guitar player. Red-hot fretwork has been a part of all his hit albums throughout the '80s and beyond. Although he goes by a different name these days, his musical mastery remains the same.

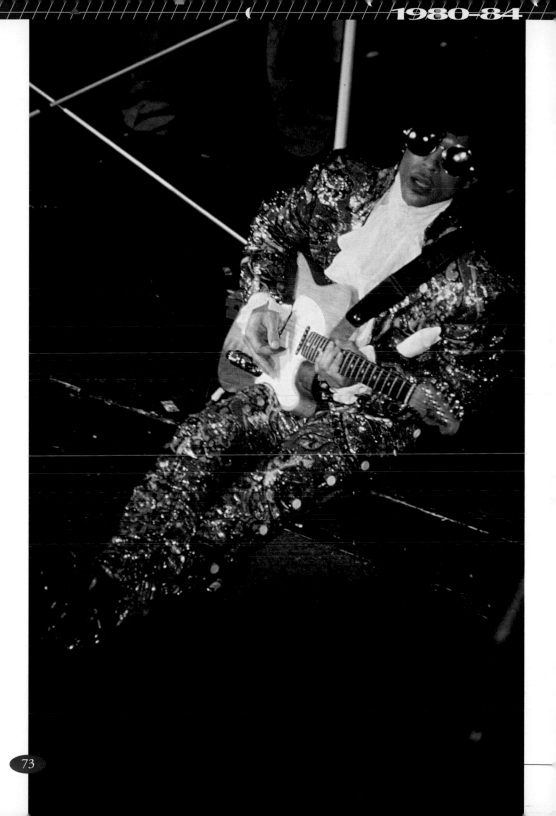

The Clash Rock the Cashbox

The Clash were one of the original punk groups that survived into the early '80s, propelled by their critically acclaimed turn-of-the-decade double album *London Calling*. From the earliest days of the band, Clash frontman Joe Strummer played a series of battered Telecasters, usually heavily stenciled and stickered with political slogans. Strummer's rhythm guitar style was equally as influenced by the scratchy chop of reggae as by the adrenaline roar of punk. Rockabilly was also an important source of inspiration for Strummer and lead guitarist Mick Jones. In the '80s the Clash broke through to a more mainstream audience. With *Combat Rock* (1982) they began to incorporate American rap sounds into their approach. The results can be heard on what is probably their best-known hit in America, "Rock the Casbah." Though they broke up shortly thereafter, the Clash are fondly remembered today. Their deeply committed political stance and powerful rock performances led one contemporary critic to call them "The only band that matters."

Three Birds (with Two Stones)

Guitar history was made in 1983 at the ARMS concerts, staged in London and four U.S. cities. The events, held to benefit victims of multiple sclerosis, brought together three of the most influential guitarists of the rock era—and former Yardbirds all: Jimmy Page, Eric Clapton, and Jeff Beck, shown here at Madison Square Garden. The rhythm section included Rolling Stones Bill Wyman and Charlie Watts. Steve Winwood played as well. The events were organized by former Small Face Ronnie Lane, who suffers from MS. Beyond uniting some of rock's greatest talents, ARMS helped set the trend for rock-related charity concerts in the '80s.

An African Monarch with an All-American Guitar

Descended from a royal family of the Yoruba tribe in Nigeria, guitarist and singer King Sunny Ade ignited the world beat explosion with his 1983 album *Ju Ju Music.*

Released and enthusiastically promoted by Island Records, the record gave many Westerners their very first taste of modern African music. What really surprised American and European listeners was the preponderance of electric guitars in ju ju music—not only electric Spanish guitars, but pedal steel as well! And lo and behold, when King Sunny Ade and his African Beats toured America in '83, Ade was playing a Fender Telecaster, and many of his band were also heavily Fender-equipped.

Guitar started entering traditional African music as early as the 1950s, taking its place alongside African instruments like the talking drum and mbira (thumb piano). Many African styles besides ju ju—including Zairean soukous, South African mbanqua, and Kenyan benga—are all extremely guitar-oriented. It's not unusual to have three, four, or five electric guitarists in a band, each playing a different line. The complex arrangements demand the kind of clean, clear guitar sounds provided by single-coil pickups in general and Fender guitars in particular.

The Sultan of Shred

The Avatar of Astounding Arpeggios, Swedish guitarist Yngwie Malmsteen was the figurehead of the neoclassical shred phenomenon of the '80s. His solo albums flummoxed fans of fancy fretwork with their dazzling displays of tapped arpeggios, lightning licks, and vertiginous dive bombs. "I love the sound of the Strat," says Yngwie of his instrument of choice. "It's my one and only sound. I got my first Strat when I was 20 years old. I've been a Strat man ever since."

Malmsteen was still a teenager working in a guitar shop in Sweden when he discovered what became one trademark of his custom Strats: their scalloped necks: "A guy came into the shop with a 16th-century lute. And instead of frets, the fingerboard was carved away so that the tip of the wood would act as a fret. I just thought it looked so nice, I tried it on a guitar." In 1993 Fender came out with the Yngwie Malmsteen Signature Series Stratocaster, embodying all the custom features found on the guitarist's own '71 Strat.

Platinum Touch

Here we find session guitar ace Steve Lukather in his natural habitat: strumming a Strat on an L.A. studio sofa, surrounded by gold and platinum records. All through the early '80s, Lukather was on an incredible roll, playing sessions for stars like Michael Jackson, Diana Ross, Elton John, Boz Skaggs, and Joni Mitchell. During this period he estimates he was playing an average of 20 sessions a week, and that he's performed on somewhere between 500 and 700 albums.

While this was going on, Lukather was also running hot with his own band, Toto, an amalgam of top L.A. session cats who grew up together in the suburban San Fernando Valley. Toto scored big with hits like "Hold the Line," "Rosanna," "Make Believe," and "Africa." They swept the 1983 Grammies, carrying home six awards.

Lukather's polished guitar style played a big role in forging what's been called the "818 Area Code Sound" (818 being the phone exchange for the San Fernando Valley)—a slick, breezy style that formed the soundtrack for the high life in L.A. during the affluent early '80s.

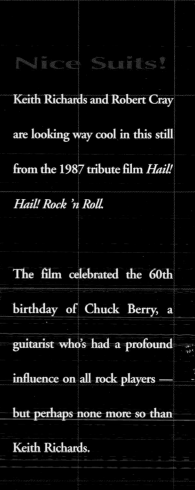

Nice Suits!

Keith Richards and Robert Cray are looking way cool in this still from the 1987 tribute film *Hail! Hail! Rock 'n Roll.*

The film celebrated the 60th birthday of Chuck Berry, a guitarist who's had a profound influence on all rock players — but perhaps none more so than Keith Richards.

David Bowie to Stevie Ray Vaughan: "Let's Dance!"

Noted for his savvy choice of sidemen, David Bowie first became aware

of Stevie Ray Vaughan via a memorable performance Vaughan and his

band Double Trouble gave at the 1982 Montreux Festival. Still fairly

unknown at the time, Vaughan was quickly enlisted to play on Bowie's

1983 hit album *Let's Dance*. Stevie Ray's own debut album, *Texas Flood*,

came out later that year.

Bowie, Vaughan, and producer/guitarist Nile Rodgers smile for the

camera during a break in the *Let's Dance* sessions.

There's Only One Chrissy

American-born Chrissy Hynde moved to London, became a rock journalist, and, in 1979, started the Pretenders. As the group's singer, songwriter, and guitarist, Hynde created a smart, sassy brand of guitar pop that has maintained its consistently high quality despite frequent personnel changes within the band's ranks. Chrissy is rarely seen without a Fender Telecaster and at least one article of tight black clothing.

Ballad of an Outlaw

West Texan Waylon Jennings played bass in the last lineup of Buddy Holly's Crickets before striking out on his own in the '60s. For years he fought the Nashville system for control of his own music, which he finally attained in the '70s. His hard-won freedom enabled him to spearhead the "outlaw" movement in country music. Eschewing the slickness of Nashville's countrypolitan establishment, outlaws like Jennings favored simple, direct arrangements and deeply personal songs—ideals that were well served by Waylon's resonant voice and scrappy, chicken pickin' Telecaster style. By the early '80s, Jennings' place at the top of the outlaw pantheon was secure, thanks to his own records and his many fine collaborations with Willie Nelson.

fender's latest decade

1985-95

Retro-mania hit America in a big way in the mid '80s. There was an outbreak of passionate interest in '50s furniture, diners, architecture, wristwatches, cars,...and of course guitars. The collectible guitar market went through the roof as baby boomers reached affluent middle age and clamored to purchase stylish symbols of their rebellious youth. Needless to say, appreciation for classic Fender guitars hit a new height at this time. Leo Fender's little post-WWII start-up company had become a great American tradition.

And in March of 1985, the guardianship of that tradition was assumed by Bill Schultz and a team of investors, who purchased Fender Musical Instruments

from CBS for $12.5 million (half a million less than CBS paid Leo Fender for the company). In the massive reorganization that followed, Schultz and his team persisted in their dual vision of Fender. That is, they continued to cultivate Fender's classic past while also seeking ways to innovate for the future. Nineteen eighty-six saw the introduction of the Fender American Standard Strat, a distillation of all the most popular modifications that players had made on the original Strat design down through the years. Small-but-effective mods like the five-position pickup switch had become *de facto* Strat standards. Now they could be purchased "stock." But at the very same time the American Standard Strat was in the works, Fender was also

cultivating relationships with innovative designers like Don Lace and Trev Wilkinson. As a result, Lace Sensor pickups and Wilkinson roller nut bridges both made their debut on the Fender Strat Plus in 1986.

In short, Fender entered the age of post-modern marketing. The past became a commodity in the mid '80s. Whether the product was a Coke, a Barbie doll, or a Fender guitar, the consumer could opt for the classic or the new version. And at mid decade, shoppers were buying "classic" in a big way. It's something that happens at the end of most centuries. People seek the security of the past.

As a corollary to the nostalgia boom, the middle '80s also saw a strong revival of

interest in traditional American roots music—country and blues. At the level of mass culture, this took the form of "country hunk" sensations like Billy Ray Cyrus. But there was also room for the more schooled neotraditionalism of a Dwight Yoakam, Vince Gill, and k.d. lang. And in blues, the mid '80s and early '90s saw the rise of bright new talents like Robert Cray and Stevie Ray Vaughan. These artists were quick to bring *their* mentors into the limelight, introducing a whole new audience to blues masters like Buddy Guy and Albert Collins. In honky tonks and stadiums everywhere, the time-honored sounds of Fender guitars, basses, and amps were ringing out.

But the retro vibe wasn't confined to the baby boom generation. At the turn of the '90s, alternative rock became a mainstream musical style and a predominant voice of youth culture. And the power that put alternative on the map was the good old sound of heavy rock guitar. Nineties alternative guitarists like Kurt Cobain of Nirvana and Billy Corgan of Smashing Pumpkins looked back to *their* childhoods in the early '70s and the heyday of metal bands like Led Zeppelin and Black Sabbath. This influence got mixed in with punk, and the result was something called *grunge*. Grunge can perhaps best be described as the sound of a Fender Jaguar or Jazzmaster into a Fender Bassman with everything cranked to 10. As grunge came to the fore,

Fender's newly established Custom Shop began collaborating with players like Cobain, incorporating their vision into the grand tradition of electric guitar playing.

Grunge peaked in 1994 with the sad death of Kurt Cobain. In the time since then there's been a neopunk revival, a "new wave of new wave," and an explosion of exciting new sounds the likes of which have never been heard before. The continued presence of Fender gear among the artists who are shaping tomorrow's music suggests that, no matter how quickly musical styles change, the need for great-sounding guitars, basses, and amps remains constant. Leo Fender passed away in 1991, but the

company that bears his name is going stronger than ever.

While the past has been a hot commodity in recent years, the future seems likely to be the big seller of the late '90s, as everyone scrambles to get on the information superhighway and set up shop in cyberspace. In this electronic future, the entire musical past will be present and available as it's never been before. It seems like the perfect place for Fender Musical Instruments to spend its *next* 50 years.

Clapton at Live Aid

The mid '80s were a time of turbulence and triumph for Eric Clapton, marked by the dissolution of his marriage to Patti Boyd (formerly Mrs. George Harrison), the start of a new relationship, and the birth of a son whose time on earth was fated to be brief. Clapton's 1986 album *August* (produced by Phil Collins) proved to be his first Top 3 release in the U.K. in 12 years. It was the start of the third big crest of Clapton's career, a ground swell that would lead to the history-making *24 Nights* residency at the Royal Albert Hall in London and E.C.'s big Grammy sweep in '93. Along the way, in 1988, Clapton became the fitting recipient of the very first signature model Stratocaster to be produced by Fender's newly established Custom Shop.

Clapton was naturally one of the rock giants asked to participate in Live Aid. This high-tech humanitarian media event, which took place on July 13, 1985, was organized by ex-Boomtown Rats leader Bob Geldof to benefit victims of a catastrophic famine in Ethiopia. His idea was to stage two simultaneous star-studded concerts linked via satellite television signals. And so for 16 hours, 72,000 concertgoers at Wembley Stadium in London mingled electronically with 90,000 at J.F.K. Stadium in Philadelphia. An additional 1.5 million people watched the event on television sets across the world. A stunning array of stars performed at Live Aid; The Who, Led Zeppelin, Black Sabbath, and Status Quo even reunited for the event. The day was a resounding financial success, and Geldof was knighted for his work.

Tele-Kinetic

The late Danny Gatton knew the Telecaster inside and out. Not only was he an absolute master of his chosen instrument's maple fretboard, he was also a veteran hot-rodder who customized his Teles with an unerring ear for tone. Bending strings into muscular harmonic clusters, Gatton blended six-string styles in a heady brew that's best described by the title of an early album of his: *Hillbilly Jazz.* Gatton first took to the Telecaster in 1971, inspired by his fellow guitar legend the late Roy Buchanan. His very first Tele was an old '52 that he received in payment for a session, and which he immediately retrofitted with a '55 neck. He played a variety of personally modified early-'50s Teles down through the years, into vintage Fender Bassmans, Twins, and Vibroverbs. In 1993 he switched to the Fender Signature Series Telecaster he designed for Fender, and which can be heard on his album *88 Elmira Street.*

Here's Gatton in action on New Year's Eve 1991 at the Hyatt Crystal City in Maryland, as captured on film by his long-time friend and pickup designer, Joe Barden.

Born in the U.S.A.

The mid '80s were a high point for Bruce Springsteen.

His album *Born in the U.S.A.* took him to a new height

of mass popularity, as his marathon live performances

hit a new level of intensity. Down through the years,

the Boss has remained true-blue to his all-American

Fender Esquire.

Warmup for Lollapalooza?

Jane's Addiction ignited a new moment in youth culture by blending heavy metal riffology with the aquatic, chorusy guitar textures of mid-'80s post-punk groups like Bauhaus and the Cure. Here they're seen in full cry at an L.A. night spot in 1987, a year before being signed to Warner Bros. and releasing their influential major-label debut, *Nothing's Shocking*. Guitarist Dave Navarro (far left) went on to join the Red Hot Chili Peppers after Jane's Addiction broke up. Strident, androgynous singer Perry Farrell is the organizer of the annual Lollapalooza rock festival and coined the phrase "alternative nation."

Flag Wavers

Multi-platinum Irish rockers U2 surprised denizens of the financial district in San Francisco when they staged an impromptu free lunchtime concert at the Justin Herman Plaza on November 11, 1987.

Announced just two hours in advance, the show nevertheless drew 20,000 spectators. The event was filmed for U2's celebrated *Rattle and Hum* documentary. During the closing number, "Pride (In the Name of Love)," U2 singer Bono climbed atop the Vaillancourt Fountain and spray-painted the slogans "Stop the Traffic" and "Rock and Roll" onto the structure. This gesture was *not* appreciated by city authorities, then in the midst of a major "stop the graffiti" campaign. The singer wound up complying with mayor Dianne Feinstein's demand that he make a public apology.

90

Los Lobos Play the Grammies

Los Lobos expanded our idea of American roots music by blending the *conjunto* sounds of their Mexican-American heritage with some of the gutsiest rock 'n' roll and blues sounds to be heard on either side of the border. Formed in Los Angeles in 1974, the band played bars, parties, and weddings until breaking through to an international audience in the mid '80s. Collectively and individually, they're highly sought-after musicians who've worked with the likes of Paul Simon, John Lee Hooker, Bob Dylan, Elvis Costello, and Ry Cooder. Here they're seen performing at the 1988 Grammy Awards.

But Which One's Which?

"The Fire and the Fury Tour" of 1989 united two of the all-time greatest guitarists: Jeff Beck and Stevie Ray Vaughan. Beck returned to the limelight and entered a new musical phase in '89, with his formidable album *Guitar Shop*. That very same year, SRV bounced back from a bout of illness and drug abuse with the breathtaking *In Step*. The two supreme Strat slingers were clearly in step for this show at Madison Square Garden.

The Godfather of Punk

As leader of the Velvet Underground in the mid-to-late '60s, Lou Reed drew the blueprint for what would become punk and post-punk alternative music. The Velvets had it all: a brooding bohemian sensibility, Reed's stark urban-realist lyrics, and a relentlessly experimental guitar approach that could embrace everything from total cacophony to passages of heartrending gentleness and clarity. The turn of the current decade marked one of many high points in Reed's prolific career. His 1989 album *New York* is a lean, angry masterpiece and one of his best-selling discs ever. The following year he reunited with fellow former Velvet John Cale to pay tribute to their friend and mentor Andy Warhol on the beautiful *Songs for Drella*. And in 1993 the Velvet Underground played three glorious reunion gigs in Paris. Rock 'n' roll would not be what it is today without Lou Reed compositions like "Sweet Jane," "All Tomorrow's Parties," "Venus in Furs," "Rock and Roll," and "Take a Walk on the Wild Side." Lyricists of Reed's caliber are typically not guitar fiends, but Lou's the exception. Notoriously obsessive about tone and equipment, Reed switched to Fender guitars around the time of *New York*.

Two Classics

Eric Johnson's guitar style is as trim and timeless as the lines of this '57 Chevy. Johnson's 1990 album *Ah Via Musicom* satisfied the appetite of the era for dazzling technique, but also reintroduced something that had been sadly missing: tone. Johnson's quest for the perfect guitar tone led him to an obvious conclusion: the Fender Stratocaster.

94

Stevie Ray's Last Jam

Even if the evening hadn't ended in tragedy, it still would've been a night to remember. The stage at Alpine Valley in Wisconsin was crowded with blues guitar titans on Sunday night, August 26, 1990. Stevie Ray Vaughan, Eric Clapton, Buddy Guy, Robert Cray, and Jimmie Vaughan were *all* up there, wailing before a crowd of 25,000 on the blues standard "Sweet Home Chicago." After the show, Vaughan boarded a five-seat helicopter that was to transport him from the venue to Meigs Field in Chicago. He never made it. The helicopter struck a hillside in dense fog. Everyone aboard was killed.

Vaughan was just 35 when he died, but he'd already established himself as the premier blues guitarist of his generation—a man who'd brought the blues into modern times while remaining deeply rooted in its past. In the process, he won the blues a whole new generation of fans. Though he's no longer with us, Stevie and his road-worn sunburst Strat will always be remembered.

fender's latest decade

It's a Guy Thing

Occupying the regal seat inside the House of Blues in Hollywood is a man who deserves that exalted position: Buddy Guy. Eric Clapton has called him "by far and without a doubt the best guitarist alive." Over the course of a career that stretches back to the late '50s, Guy has developed a shiver-inducing blues style, punctuating his highly emotional singing with frenetic bursts of sheer electric guitar genius. As a session guitarist for Chess Records, Buddy got to cut tracks with immortals like Muddy Waters and Howlin' Wolf. His duets with harmonica wizard Junior Wells are the stuff that blues legends are made of. Jimi Hendrix studied Guy's playing obsessively, as have many other guitarist down through the years.

The '90s have brought much-deserved recognition for Buddy Guy. His 1991 LP *Damn Right, I've Got the Blues* earned scores of new admirers. Eric Clapton invited Guy to be part of the all-star blues guitar lineup for his *24 Nights* concerts at the Royal Albert Hall in 1990–91. Buddy has collected two Grammies and *Billboard*s prestigious Century Award. But it doesn't take a list of prizes to demonstrate Guy's greatness. A few notes from the man and his polka-dot Strat are all that's required.

Party Time! Excellent!

Before Beavis and Butthead, there were Wayne and Garth. Comedian Mike Myers' portrayal of Wayne on "Saturday Night Live" and in the *Wayne's World* movies caught the essence of midwestern adolescent metal dudehood. With the possible exception of his girlfriend Cassandra (played by Tia Carrere), the number one object of Wayne's desire was a gleaming white Fender Stratocaster enshrined in the local music store in his home town of Aurora, Illinois. In this still from the first *Wayne's World* film, our hero gets to spend some quality time with his dream guitar, valiantly striving to honor the posted house rule: NO "Stairway to Heaven."

Texas Twang

When he was just six years old, Lee Roy Parnell sang a song with Texas swing king Bob Wills on a radio program broadcast from Fort Worth. It was an auspicious beginning to a long and productive career. A red-hot slide player and all-around guitar ace, Parnell played in Kinky Friedman's Texas Jewboys and has performed on an impressive stack of country records by artists like Tricia Yearwood and Mary Chapin Carpenter. A fine singer and songwriter as well as a stunning guitarist, Parnell has released four albums of his own.

Look What I Got for Christmas!

Along with Kevin Shields of My Bloody Valentine, Sonic Youth have played a central role in reinventing the electric guitar for the alternative rock '90s. They achieve grainy, evocative guitar textures through their use of wild alternative tunings, unconventional playing techniques, and psychotic amounts of overdrive. Fender Jazzmasters and Jaguars are among their most favored guitars, partly because these instruments can be strummed *behind* the bridge. With an amp set to warp drive, this technique produces cascades of barbed-wire harmonics. While Sonic Youth have been around since 1982, they had a major commercial breakthrough with the brilliant *Goo* in 1990. The disc helped spark a '90s vogue for alternately tuned Jags and Jazzmasters.

Thurston Moore holds his Jazzmaster aloft for the crowd to admire at a concert at the Shoreline Amphitheater in Mountain View, California, in early 1995.

Stretched Hammstrings

Some bassists have been praised for showing how the bass can be a melodic instrument. Others for exploring the bass's rhythmic accompaniment potential. Stu Hamm does both at the same time. Hamm studied piano as a kid and figured out how to use fretboard tapping to play both the right- and left-hand parts to keyboard classics like Beethoven's "Moonlight" Sonata and Vince Guaraldi's "Peanuts" theme on the bass. It's one of the techniques that made Hamm's 1988 debut, *Radio Free Albemuth*, a landmark of bass guitar virtuosity. Hamm's agile playing on Steve Vai's *Passion and Warfare* and Joe Satriani's *Dreaming #11* shows he can keep up with the fastest guns in all guitardom. But here we see him with a few *really* close friends.

Belew + Bowie = Sound + Vision

Experimental guitarist extraordinaire Adrian Belew has performed with some of the most important artists of our era, including Frank Zappa, King Crimson, Talking Heads, Paul Simon, and Laurie Anderson. Belew first worked with David Bowie on the latter's 1978 world tour and on his 1979 masterpiece *Lodger*. They got back together for Bowie's 1990 *Sound + Vision* tour, pictured here in an appearance at the Spectrum in Philadelphia. The panoramically perverse imagination of David Bowie found an ideal minion in Adrian Belew, whose mastery of feedback and effects can make a Fender Stratocaster sound like anything from an extraterrestrial mating call to a jailbreak at the Bronx Zoo.

Hellecaster Goes Co-Ed

Looking very "lumberjack," Jerry Donahue shares the stage with singer/songwriter Rosie Flores at the historic Palomino club in L.A. Donahue is one third of the Hellecasters, a trio of twangin' virtuosi whose ranks also include John Jorgensen and Will Ray. An American by birth, Jerry began his career playing with the legendary British folk group Fairport Convention. He went on to distinguish himself as a solo artist, session ace, and, since 1988, a full-fledged Hellecaster. And just what *is* a Hellecaster? Someone who plays the hell of out a Telecaster, what else? In guitar circles, Jerry is renowned for his stunning repertoire of double, triple, and contrary-motion string bends— a regular fretboard rodeo, all executed on his signature model Fender Custom Shop Telecaster.

fender's latest decade

Strat Buddies

Richie Sambora was inspired to start playing guitar by Eric Clapton's searing Stratocaster work on the *Layla* album. But it wasn't until Richie was recording *Slippery When Wet*—Bon Jovi's 1986 multi-platinum breakthrough album—that he began playing Strats himself. Nineteen ninety-one was a banner year for Sambora: Eric Clapton guested on his debut solo album, *Stranger in this Town*, and he collaborated with Fender on the Richie Sambora Signature Strat. Here we see Richie onstage in '91 with his hero at the Roxy in Los Angeles. The two of them got up to jam at a Buddy Guy gig, cementing a newfound friendship.

Nirvana Play Reading

Nirvana's appearance at the 1992 Reading Festival—England's prestigious alternative rock showcase—confirmed the phenomenal success of the band's 1991 album *Nevermind* and the arrival of American grunge as the predominant alternative rock sound of the early '90s. This photo, by grunge documentarian Charles Peterson, captures the vibe of that overcast, muddy late summer's day. Kurt Cobain wore a hospital gown and was brought onstage in a wheelchair—his way of mocking rumors in the British rock press that the band was breaking up because of their leader's ill health.

A left-handed guitarist, Cobain favored old Fender Jaguars and Mustangs. But since guitars were often smashed in the unbridled fury of Nirvana's live shows, Cobain was always scrambling around for lefty models of the Fender guitars he loved. Shortly before his death, he collaborated with Fender on a custom model incorporating elements of both the Jaguar and the Mustang. He called it the Jagstang.

Just two years after Nirvana's triumphant appearance at Reading, Cobain was dead by his own hand. But he occupies a permanent place in the hearts of an entire rock generation.

Rock 'n' Roll Survivors

Aerosmith lived through years of rock 'n' roll excess and early critical dismissal as Stones clones to emerge triumphant in the '90s. Honored by everyone from rappers Run D.M.C. to Wayne and Garth ("We are not worthy!"), Aerosmith were voted best band in the 1991 *Rolling Stone* music awards. Here Aerosmith rhythm guitarist Brad Whitford backs singer Steven Tyler at a 1993 gig.

Woodstock '94

The memory of the first Woodstock festival in 1969 loomed large at Woodstock '94, held on August 12–14 and attended by an estimated 300,000 people. The Red Hot Chili Peppers went on next to closing—followed by Peter Gabriel—and turned their set into a surrealistically campy tribute to Jimi Hendrix. Peppers bassist Flea brought his daughter Clara onstage to sing "The Star-Spangled Banner"—the tune with which Hendrix had closed the first Woodstock festival. Then all four Chili Peppers appeared on stage decked out in matching "Jimi Hendrix suits" (complete with Afro wigs) and ripped into "Power of Equality." All band members were equipped with Fender Squier Strats for the occasion (except for lead guitarist Dave Navarro, who played the same Strat he usually does). At the climax of the set, the Strats were trashed in an orgy of Jimi-esque tough love. As a parting gesture (see photo), drummer Chad Smith flung his Strat into a mud-drenched crowd holding candles that were supposed to be dispensed for Peter Gabriel's set but somehow got distributed prematurely.

(Inset:) Electric gypsies Anthony Kiedis and Dave Navarro beg to be 'scused while they kiss the sky.

Phair Play

Liz Phair is one of the best songwriters to emerge from the recent alternative scene. Her sharp-edged wit and killer melodic instincts prove that songcraft isn't a dead issue in the '90s. Here Liz plays her trusty Fender Musicmaster at a club gig.

Pumpkins Have Feelings Too

Leader of alternative faves Smashing Pumpkins, Billy Corgan has become an icon of Generation-X emotional vulnerability through his cryptically confessional lyrics, temper-tantrum vocals, and little-boy-lost looks. He's also one hell of a guitarist. The son of a professional guitar player, Corgan can move easily from Hendrixian psychedelia to sledgehammer metal to moments of quiet introspection on the '57 Reissue Strats and '74 Bullet Strats he prefers as his main axes. Here Billy flaunts a Strat with a tender message at the Pumpkins' Lollapalooza '95 gig in their home town of Chicago.

One of the most overtly "metal" bands to emerge from the Seattle scene, Pearl Jam took grunge straight to the top of the charts in the early '90s. The shred-influenced Strat stylings of lead man Mike McCready provide the ideal complement for rhythm guitarist Stone Gossard's slabby open tunings, making Pearl Jam's two-guitar attack a force to be reckoned with. Here McCready demonstrates his ability to smoke, play guitar, and stand on one foot—all at the same time.

Musical Matriarch

Bonnie Raitt overcame gender stereotypes to establish herself as one of the most respected slide guitar players on the rock and blues scenes. In 1995 she launched a campaign to ease the way for women guitarists of the future. The Bonnie Raitt Guitar Project is a charity program designed to place guitars in the hands of inner city girls. All royalties from Bonnie's Signature Series Stratocaster will be donated to the project. Fender will supply guitars for the program, as well as providing lessons and support through its dealer network.

Ms. Free Love

Outspoken, uninhibited, provocative, and confrontational, Courtney Love is to the '90s what Madonna was to the '80s—a cynosure of controversy, a habitual breaker of taboos. The widow of Kurt Cobain, Courtney has found success in the '90s as leader of the band Hole. Launched in Los Angeles in 1989, Hole subsequently relocated to Seattle, where they became part of that city's grunge music scene and post-feminist Riot Grrrl movement. Ms. Love is seen here with her Courtney Love Custom Shop creation.

Tribute to a Towering Texan

On May 11 and 12, 1995, the finest blues guitarists converged on Austin, Texas, to pay tribute to the late Stevie Ray Vaughan. This moment, captured by Cindy Light, comes from the second evening's tribute: a sticky hot Texas night at the Austin Music Hall. (Left to right:) Robert Cray, Buddy Guy, Jimmie Vaughan, and Eric Clapton—the four guitarists who shared the stage with Stevie Ray on the last night of his life.